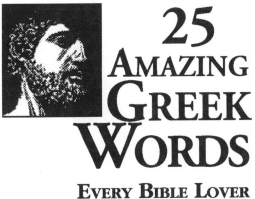

25 AMAZING GREEK WORDS

EVERY BIBLE LOVER MUST DISCOVER

Gregory A. Lint

World Library Press Inc.
Springfield, Missouri, U.S.A.

ISBN 1-884642-00-4

Published by World Library Press Inc.
2274 E. Sunshine
Springfield, Missouri 65804 U.S.A.

Printed for the glory of God.

Dedicated to
Bible lovers
everywhere.

Special thanks to:
Dr. Benny Aker
Dr. Gary B. McGee
Dr. Donald A. Johns
Jacob Trout, M.A.
and
Dr. Stanley M. Horton

Table of Contents

Introduction

Welcome to 25 Amazing Greek Words. Soon you will discover how a few Greek words can revolutionize your Bible study. You will also better understand what you hear in sermons. And you will feel more confident when sharing your own knowledge of your relationship with God.

What Can This Book Do For You?

25 Amazing Greek Words is a fascinating and helpful study of the concepts which constantly interweave throughout the New Testament. Every Bible lover needs to have a framework to build on to be able to adequately study the Bible. Scholars call this systematic theology.

With *25 Amazing Greek Words* you can discover fruitful insights to the New Testament which will enhance your understanding of God's Word. While savoring these enriching word studies, you will be learning the basic concepts necessary to launch a life-time of enjoyable Bible study.

Who Benefits From This Book?

You will find that this book has valuable information for ministers and Bible students, as well as the average layman. As you unearth the concepts of the New Testament you will quickly see why this book was named *25 Amazing Greek Words—Every Bible Lover Must Discover.* If you are a layman,

25 Amazing Greek Words will give you information
about the basic subjects in the Bible. An added
benefit is that your personal Bible study will be
enhanced as you begin to understand more about
what the New Testament writers thought about their
times. *25 Amazing Greek Words* can also help you
understand sermons better.

If you preach, but know little or no Greek, your
sermons can take on new excitement with *25 Amazing Greek Words*. You can preach with confidence
knowing that the information has been prepared
with the utmost care. All information has been
cross-checked by the most renowned sources of our
time. In addition, you will be better equipped to
step back in history, understand the thinking of the
people of that time and bring an enriched interpretation forward in time to your congregation.

Knowledge Is Your Key To Empowerment

With *25 Amazing Greek Words* you will gain
knowledge about one of history's most extraordinary languages. Many experts believe it was no
accident that God chose Greek for the original
language of the New Testament. Koine (or common) Greek is a particularly expressive language
and its beauty can be understood and appreciated by
everyone.

Some people might have you think that the
average person cannot understand Greek or that a

casual study of Greek will only mislead believers
(or at best waste your time). The Greek word for
this kind of thinking is "bologna!" Anything which
helps you understand the Bible more fully is for
everyone and is never a waste of time. You will
find that questions will arise in your adventure of
learning, but it will be worth the rich treasures you
will uncover in the process.

Learning the Words

For each word which you will be learning, this is
what to expect:

First you will see the word with a pronunciation
key to help you say the word properly. Then you
will discover the basic meanings. This will give
you a background with which to begin. Most Greek
words have several meanings with one being the
most common definition. The first part of the
definition section tells you what significance each
word had in Classical Greek literature. Many key
New Testament words had one nuance in secular
Greek writings, but took on new and powerful
significance with the exciting happenings of the
Christian Church of the first century. Some refer to
these as "born-again" words.

You will then be given a helpful way to remember this word before you launch into a New Testament study of the important concept this word
conveys. Significant Scriptures will be given and

you will be challenged to look them up in whatever Bible study tools you use. You can begin your own exploration of the Scriptures with the information found in *25 Amazing Greek Words.*

Each discussion will conclude with a sample verse that highlights the meaning. The word being translated will be in bold print. These verses have been carefully chosen to bring out the main concept of the word being discussed. Many of these verses will be quite familiar to you and will inspire you to begin a new search of a favorite passage. You will find that these simple 25 words are the keys which will unlock scriptural understanding that you might never discover in any other way.

You should reread this book as often as you like to learn at your own pace. You may not be able to memorize every word the first time through, but this is common.

Knowledge Begins With the Turn of This Page

Now it is time to get started with *25 Amazing Greek Words.* May God bless you and illuminate your heart in your study.

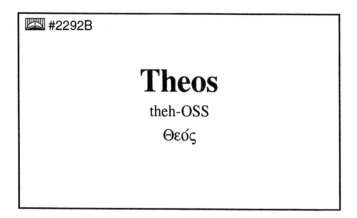

You will probably not be surprised to find that *theos* is the word used for God. What you may not know is that it can also be used to refer to false gods of the pagans. Some examples of this word referring to pagan gods are Acts 7:40 and Galatians 4:8. *Theos* is not always a specialized word like the Hebrew word *Yahweh* which only refers to the One True God.

Classical Greek naturally does not recognize the One True God in its usage. To help you remember the meaning of *theos*, think of our English word theology (the study of God).

In the New Testament, *theos* occurs hundreds of times. The name of God usually occurs with an article ("the") before it, but not always. The reason the article is sometimes omitted is to draw attention to one of God's qualities, but its omission does not take away from God's nature as the only Deity in existence. While the Son and the Holy Spirit are equally God, *theos* usually is a term reserved for the Father.

The Bible does not try to prove God's existence. The first few words in the Bible are "In the beginning, God." God is the One True God (Ephesians 4:6), yet He is three Persons (Father, Son and Spirit). He is perfect (Matthew 5:48) and holy (1 Peter 1:15-16) but loves man anyway (John 3:16). God is all-powerful, all-knowing and present everywhere.

Those who become Christians will have a change of character. The most important change is to love others with the kind of love that flows from God (I John 4:21).

Our sample verse is from Matthew 19:26.
*"With **God** all things are possible."*

#3824

Pater

pah-TEAR

Πατήρ

Pater is a noun with both literal and deeper meanings. *Pater* means "father" in many languages. It may mean the father of an individual, clan or country. In the New Testament, the nuances are much the same as in the original meanings except for one.

When we think of the word "father" in the biblical sense, we usually think of God the Father. Other meanings include Abraham, the father of the Israelite nation (John 8:39) as well as the father of a family as in the parable of the prodigal son (Luke 15). *Pater* is an example of taking an ordinary word and using it for an extraordinary meaning so that the things of heaven can be related to man. That is what makes this word a great one.

Jesus spoke of the Father many times in His teachings. He often used the phrase "My Father," but He also described God as being the Father of all believers. When He taught His disciples to pray, He told them to say, "Our Father, which art in heaven..." (Luke 11:2).

The Father is the source of all good gifts (James 1:17) including Jesus, our Savior (Romans 7:25). Because the Father created us and loves us greatly, He wants to have a close relationship with us. The work of Jesus Christ made it possible for us to call God our Father (Romans 8:15).

Our sample verse is from John 14:2.

"In My **Father's** *house are many dwelling places; if it were not so, I would have told you."*

📖 #2935

Kurios

KOOR-ee-oss

Κύριος

Kurios means "lord" or "master." This could be Lord of the universe, lord over a household or any position in between. The original meaning of *kurios* was also "lord" or "master." Its classical usage is in keeping with the New Testament meanings referring to almost any authority.

Even today, some uses still reflect this idea. England has the House of Lords. Renters have a landlord. Mostly, though, we have replaced the word lord with "owner" or "boss." This is, in fact, the way we should think of the Greek word *kurios*. To remember the meaning of *kurios*, think of travelling to England. You would probably be curious to see The House of Lords.

In the New Testament, there are a few uses of *kurios* which do not refer to God. These are just like the original meanings in Classical Greek. The most common examples would be in the parables about owners of vineyards, farms or some other possession. You can find *kurios* used this way in Matthew 20:8.

Paul called himself a slave many times to emphasize that he was obligated to obey the Lord. This is what Paul was referring to when he wrote, "You are not your own; you have been bought with a price" (1 Corinthians 6:19, 20). The Bible teaches that a mark of a Christian is obedience to God instead of to Satan.

The most common meaning of *kurios* is in reference to Jesus or the entire Godhead. The lordship of Jesus Christ is one of the central messages of the Bible, so this usage occurs hundreds of times in the New Testament. (1 Corinthians 16:23). Jesus is both Savior and Lord!

Our sample verse is from Philippians 2:11.
"Every tongue will confess that Jesus Christ is **Lord***, to the glory of God."*

#2400

Iesous

Ee-ay-SOOS

Ἰησοῦς

Iesous is the name for Jesus. It's the Greek way of saying the Hebrew word *Yeshua*, or, as we say, Joshua. Jesus is simply the English version of *Iesous*. *Iesous* comes from the Hebrew verb meaning "to save" or "to deliver." His name reflects His earthly mission and His eternal saving power.

"Jesus" is not simply a name that was given to the baby of Mary and Joseph, because it was a common Hebrew name. It speaks of the character of God before time began. Jesus means "Savior." His name was especially chosen by God because of the mission which Jesus had (Matthew 1:21). That mission was to make a bridge to God by way of the cross to enable man to get back to God and avoid death. The Bible clearly teaches that the only way to salvation is to accept Jesus as Savior and Lord (Acts 4:12).

Iesous is often found in the New Testament combined with the titles of Jesus. Some of these are Jesus Christ, Christ Jesus or Lord Jesus. These titles reflect His authority and anointing. Read Psalm 2 about Jesus' authority and Messiahship. One day, everyone will stand before God and proclaim the lordship of Jesus (Philippians 2:10-11).

Our sample verse is from Matthew 1:21.
"You shall call His name, '**Jesus**,*' for He will save His people from their sins."*

#5382

Christos

Cree-STOSS

Χριστός

Christos is a word of great magnitude. It is equal to the Hebrew word *Messias* (Messiah) which means "savior," or "deliverer." In Classical Greek, it is apparent that the Greeks understood the majesty of *Christos*, because they used it in titles for rulers and other men of distinction. Because of the anticipation of the Jewish Messiah, this word was important to the Hebrew people. By removing the last two letters, the English version of *Christos* became "Christ."

Many times literal meanings have cast an interesting light on the meaning of a word, but do not really tell its actual connotation. In this case, the literal translation does give us an exciting and accurate picture. The literal meaning of *Christos* is "anointed one."

This name of Jesus occurs in almost every Book of the New Testament. When *Christos* is used, it continually points out that Jesus is that Great Deliverer Who had been awaited since the time of Adam. Many deliverers of the Jewish people came before Jesus. The judges are prime examples. Outside of the Old and New Testaments, the Maccabean family were zealous warriors for the Jewish cause. But only One can deliver man from his sin—Jesus Christ.

Our sample verse is from Matthew 16:16. *"Simon Peter replied, 'You are the* **Christ**, *the Son of the living God.'"*

📖 #4011

Pneuma

NEW-ma

Πνεῦμα

Pneuma is a noun which is usually translated "spirit." It can also mean "wind" or "breath." We get our English word pneumonia from *pneuma*. A person with pneumonia must draw breath to bring wind into his lungs, or his body will surely give up its spirit. Originally, the Greeks thought of the *pneuma* as that part of man which was not material and was, therefore, the good part of man or the essence of man which was trapped in a material body. According to the Greeks, there were four basic elements in the world—earth, wind, fire and water. The wind or the air is what gave man his life-force. The Bible tells us that God breathed the breath of life into Adam.

In the New Testament, the word *pneuma* is

usually translated "spirit" and can refer to God's Spirit or man's (Compare Ephesians 4:30 and 1 Thessalonians 5:23). Man's spirit is the source of his feelings and will (Matthew 5:3). It is also the facet which communes with God (Romans 8:16).

In the Gospel of John, there are some very important discussions by Jesus about the significance of *pneuma*. In John 3:5, Jesus tells Nicodemus that to enter the kingdom of God, one must be born of water (natural birth) and of the Spirit. In John 4:24, Jesus told the woman at the well that God is Spirit, and those who want to worship Him must do so in spirit and in truth. According to Jesus, the material things of this world pale in comparison to the things of the Spirit .

Our sample verse is from Romans 8:16.
"This same **Spirit** *testifies to our* **spirit** *that we are God's children."*

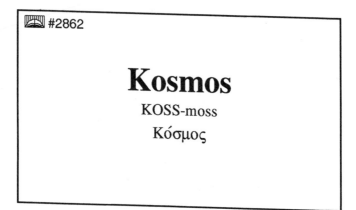

📖 #2862

Kosmos
KOSS-moss
Κόσμος

Kosmos is a word that may already be familiar to you as "cosmos." We usually use the word today to mean the entire universe. This is the origin of the word "cosmic." It is interesting that in Classical Greek, the noun *kosmos* could refer to construction. This implies the belief that the world did not happen by accident.

The meaning which we normally think of when we hear the word *kosmos* is used in the New Testament, but the general meaning is the planet Earth or the earth and everything in it.

When the New Testament uses the word *kosmos*, the implied meanings are much the same as when we use the word "world." In Matthew 5:14, *kosmos* means the people in the world or mankind. Here

Jesus makes an important statement to his disciples about being the right kind of influence to those around them. Romans 1:8 is an example of *kosmos* meaning "the world" as in the planet earth. Matthew 25:34 is a good example of *kosmos* being used to mean the entire universe.

Our sample verse is from Colossians 1:16. *"For through Him all things were created, both in the heavens and on* **earth.** *"*

📖 #32

Angelos

ON-geh-loss

Ἄγγελος

Angelos is Greek for "angel" or "messenger." It looks and sounds much like our English word "angel," so it is easy to remember. But it can be translated "demon" when referring to the fallen one third of the angelic force which do service for Satan (Jude 6). Angels were around before man was. To help you remember the meaning of this word, notice that "angel" is *angelos* without the last two letters.

From ancient times, this word has meant "messenger." The ancient Greeks believed that the responsibility of Hermes, one of their gods, was to protect messengers. (He was the guy with little wings on his feet). Messengers of ancient times were great runners used to running many miles. They would think of the Boston marathon as a light day's work.

In the Bible, the word *angelos* usually means the angels which serve God (Mark 13:32). They are often sent as messengers such as the ones sent to Zacharias, the father of John the Baptist (Luke 1:11) and to Mary and Joseph, the earthly parents of Jesus (Matthew 1). This word can also refer to human messengers such as the *angelos* of one of the churches in Revelation 1-3. In this special passage in Scripture, the meaning of *angelos* probably refers to an area leader or a pastor—the human messenger of God for a local group of believers.

Rather than a promotion for humans after death, angels are really specially created beings which carry out the will of God. Some bring messages from God such as those who proclaimed Jesus' birth (Luke 2:10). Others are guardians of believers or places (Hebrews 1:14). Some angels have the auspicious assignment of staying near the throne of God declaring His holiness (Rev. 7:11).

Our sample verse is from Acts 10:3.
"About the ninth hour of the day,
Cornelius clearly saw an **angel** *of God."*

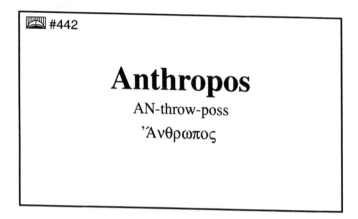

Anthropos is a noun which, as you may have already guessed, means "man" or "mankind." To help you recall the meaning of this word, remember that the modern word "anthropology" (the study of man) comes from this Greek word.

Even though *anthropos* is used to show that man is more than animal, the usage of the word also describes man as less than divine. But the Greeks still put a lot of emphasis on man. The ancient olympic games were an exhibition of the human body's achievements and capabilities. This was emphasized even more so than today. Losing was more than disappointing in the original olympics, it was shameful. The Greeks also placed a different philosophical emphasis on man than we do today.

Man was understood as a part of the unseen world, his soul being trapped in matter which was viewed as evil.

The New Testament changed the view of man from this pagan philosophy to the view which God intended from the beginning. The word *anthropos* occurs hundreds of times in the New Testament. The Bible uses *anthropos* in the ordinary sense most of the time (Matthew 20:14). But when it is used in the sense of "mankind," some important teaching is recorded in the pages of Scripture. Man was created to worship God. Sin separated man from God, but man has been provided with a way back to God through Jesus who became a man and gave His life to save us from our sins (Romans 5:17).

Our sample verse is from Hebrews 9:27.
"It is appointed to **man** *once to die,*
and then the judgment."

Hamartia is a Greek word meaning "sin" or anything associated with sin. Today, the word "sin" often brings to mind some degree of moral wrongness. But originally this was not the case.

Early Greeks associated *hamartia* with civil offenses or honest mistakes. Not until the New Testament writings was the implication of moral guilt implied in this Greek word. So today's English word "sin" is fairly accurate in describing the meaning which the New Testament places on the word *hamartia*.

You may have noticed the first two syllables of this word sound like our English word "hammer." A sledge hammer is used to drive a wedge and split wood for the fireplace. Use this to help you remember that sin—*hamartia*—drives a wedge between God and man.

Most often when *hamartia* is used in the New Testament, it refers to man's plight of being separated from God (Hebrews 2:17) and being in slavery to sin (John 8:34). *Hamartia* occurs more in Romans and Hebrews than in any other Books, and can be found in nearly every Book of the New Testament. The purpose of calling attention to man's sin in the Bible is easy to see. Such discussions are always followed by relating the way to get rid of sin and get back in right relationship with God.

Our sample verse is from I John 1:9.
"If we confess our **sins***, He is faithful and true to forgive us of our* **sins** *and to cleanse us from all unrighteousness."*

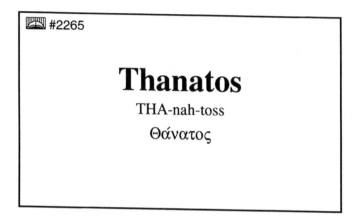

Thanatos

THA-nah-toss

Θάνατος

Thanatos is a noun which means "death." *Thanatos* can have a literal or spiritual meaning.

In Classical Greek, *thanatos* only refers to physical death or the act of dying, etc. The New Testament uses this common meaning, but it also includes the spiritual meaning. A common misunderstanding about death which has come to us through Greek thought is that death is a cessation of existence. While we know this is not the case, we often, as Westerners, think of death in this manner. To help you recall this word, remember that a general who is marching into battle plans to gain a victory, rather than a loss causing his troops to suffer death.

The New Testament often uses the word *thanatos* in a literal manner. However, the figurative usages which refer to spiritual death are most dynamic.

All men will be raised from the dead and be judged (Hebrews 9:27). But death has been conquered by Jesus' resurrection; so we can pass from death to life by accepting the Lord (1 John 3:14). Revelation 20 speaks of Death giving up the dead for the final judgment. Read this passage, and imagine this awesome scene.

Our sample verse is from 1 Corinthians 15:55.
*"O **death**, where is your victory?*
*O **death** where is your sting?"*

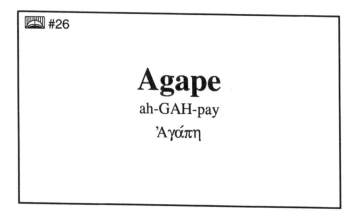

Agape
ah-GAH-pay
Ἀγάπη

Interestingly enough, the word *agape* is virtually non-existent until the New Testament. This well-known Greek word has actually become an English word today, simply being carried over from the Greek language. You may already know that the general meaning of *agape* is "love." Think of *agape* as an unsung hero in ancient Greece which was given a new purpose in New Testament writings.

The Bible discusses many kinds of love. You may have heard that *agape* is the type of love that comes from God. This is usually the case, but *agape* can also mean just the opposite, as in Matthew 24:12. In this verse, Jesus says that in the last days "the love of many will grow cold." This is not the enduring kind of love that comes from God. And, once in a while, *agape* can mean "benevolence" (Revelation 2:19) or "love-feast" (Jude 12).

The Bible has a lot to say about love. God showed the greatest love of all by sending Jesus to die on the cross for us when we were still sinners (Romans 5:8). The love of God in our hearts allows us to love God with everything we have. It also enables us to love our neighbor, our enemy and our brother.

Our sample verse is from Romans 5:8.
"God demontrated His **love** *toward us in this way— while we were still sinners, Christ died for us."*

🏛 #129

Haima

HAY-mah

Αἷμα

The only translation in the New Testament for *haima* is "blood." But there is deep meaning attached beyond just physical blood. It is interesting that in ancient Greece, blood was important to pagan religions. Animal and even human sacrifices were offered to false gods. A good way to remember the meaning of *haima* is to remember that it sounds like the word "aim." A hunter tries to take aim and draw the life-blood of the animal.

In the Bible, *haima* is used in reference to Old Testament sacrifices (Hebrews 9:12), the blood of a murdered people (Luke 11:51) and the blood of Jesus which atones for man's sin (Ephesians 2:19).

Hebrews 9 contains the word *haima* eleven times. In this classic discussion about atonement for sin, the theme of the Book of Hebrews is brought to its pinnacle. The theme of the Book is "better." Hebrews 9:13, 14 tells us that the Old Testament sacrifices could ceremonially cleanse a person on the outside, but the blood of Jesus cleanses on the inside bringing new life. You might want to look up Hebrews 9 to study *haima* further.

Salvation through the blood of Jesus on the cross is clearly the central message of the entire Bible. Because of this, there is not a more important Greek word. The blood of Jesus is the purchasing agent which brings man from death to life (Ephesians 1:7).

Our sample verse is from Romans 3:25.
"God presented him [Jesus] as a sacrifice of atonement through faith in his **blood.** *"*

📖 #1236

Diatheke

dee-ah-THAY-kay

Διαθήκη

Diatheke is a noun which can be translated "contract," "testament" or "covenant." Today, "covenant" is the most popular translation, but "contract" is probably more accurate in terms of today's English. In ancient times, the idea of *diatheke* was a last will and testament or some type of legal contract. To remember this word, think of a lawyer asking his colleague, "Did they okay the contract?"

The names of the two parts of the Bible come from this word and from Jesus' statements at the last supper. The Old and New Testaments are the Old and New *Diatheke*. Some prefer to call them the "Older and Newer Testaments" to show that the Old Testament is still the Word of God (Mark 14:22-25). Jesus told His disciples (although they did not quite understand until after the resurrection) that the Old Testament requirements were going to be fulfilled by His death on the cross. No longer would mankind have the burden of trying to be righteous by the Law.

The type of covenant or contract between God and man is not an agreement reached between two parties, but an offer made by God which man can either accept or reject. The acceptance of this contract or *diatheke* means that the party consenting is obligated to obey the directions of the party making the contract. Interestingly, Deuteronomy follows such a format. This is called a Suzerain contract. In the time of Moses a conquering king would make a deal with the people that lost the battle. If the people obeyed the new king, they would benefit. If they disobeyed, they faced severe consequences.

Today, God makes an outstanding offer to man. If man will surrender everything to God, God will take away his sin and give blessings on earth and an eternal heavenly home.

Our sample verse is from 1 Corinthians 11:25. *"In the same way, He took the cup also, after supper, saying, 'This cup is the new* **covenant** *in My blood: do this, as often as you drink it, in remembrance of Me.'"*

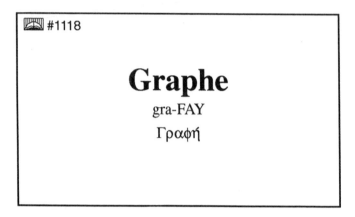

#1118

Graphe

gra-FAY

Γραφή

Graphe is a noun which means "writing." Today it is still used in the English language for words such as autograph, photograph and graphic. To help you remember the meaning of *graphe* recall that the "lead" in a pencil, something used for writing, is called graphite.

In English, a graph is a specially prepared document to help us understand a concept or information. This is a good way of remembering the meaning of *graphe*, because "writing," as it is referred to in the New Testament by this Greek word, is "the Scripture." In fact, that is the way *graphe* is always translated. The Scriptures are God's graph—His specially prepared document for helping us understand. The most common use of *graphe* in the New Testament is to refer to a quotation from the Old Testament. Often, the New Testament will point out a meaningful Scriptural prophecy from the Old Testament and explain the fulfillment of its earlier revelation.

Now remember that the "Scripture" which the New Testament refers to is actually the Old Testament, since the New Testament was in the process of being formed at the time. The most important function of the Scripture is to give special revelation to man so he can be reconciled to God. The Bible was given by the inspiration of God (literally, the Scriptures were "God-breathed" [2 Timothy 3:16]).

Our sample verse is in 2 Timothy 3:16.
"All **Scripture** *is given by inspiration of God."*

#4843

Soteria

so-tay-REE-ah

Σωτηρία

Soteria is a noun which means "salvation." In ancient times, *soteria* was sometimes used in a general sense, such as to keep someone or prevent someone from being harmed. The pagan gods were looked to for protection and for salvation from dangerous situations. But the Greeks' search for immortality was only a dream. Since sin was not thought of as moral wrongness, salvation was not thought of as deliverance from man's moral plight. The Greek word *soteria* gives us our word "soteriology," the study of the doctrine of salvation. To remember the meaning of *soteria*, think of a salvation prayer which asks God, "So tear me away from my sin."

The New Testament uses the word *soteria* in a

much fuller sense. Man is a fallen creature because of Adam's sin, therefore everyone is in need of salvation to prevent destruction. The Bible teaches that salvation is a gift of God which provides man with eternal life and freedom from his former life of sin (Romans 6:23). *Soteria* is also a restoration of man to a right relationship with God (Romans 5:1).

The Bible also teaches that Jesus is the only way to salvation. As Paul explains in Romans, no one gets saved by trying to follow a list of do's and don'ts. The Law which God gave to Moses could point out man's guiltiness, but could not provide a permanent solution for sin (Galatians 3:21). The penalty for sin is death. It took a sinless sacrifice to make a way for man to escape (1 Peter 1:19, 20). Jesus defeated sin and death by dying a sacrificial death and rising again (1 Corinthians 15:55-57). Only in this way could one Man die for the world (Galatians 3:22, Romans 5:17).

Our sample verse is from Acts 4:12.
*"And there is **salvation** in no one else; for there is no other name under heaven that has been given among men, by which we must be saved."*

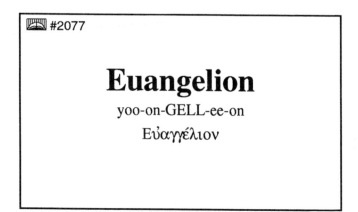

#2077

Euangelion
yoo-on-GELL-ee-on
Εὐαγγέλιον

Euangelion is a noun which means "gospel" or "good news." Essentially, the gospel is God's good news to mankind. Secular usage included only the meaning of "good news." In ancient times, the Greek went to the temple to get some good news from the gods. He might offer an extra sacrifice in order to receive a good piece of information from the gods by way of oracle. We get our English word "evangelize" or "evangelist" (one who brings the Good News) from *euangelion*.

In the Bible we know that the gospel message is the central message. Paul uses the word *euangelion* more than any other writer. He often describes his state of physical abasement as a small price for communicating the gospel to the world (Romans 8:18). Through Christ, he could do anything (Philippians 4:13). That is, there was nothing that Paul could not do, with Christ's help, to obey his calling—preaching the Gospel.

The first four books of the New Testament are named "gospels." This indicates their purpose. They are doing more than simply relating a biography of Jesus' life. You may be interested to know that scholars often refer to Matthew, Mark, Luke and John as evangelists.

Our sample verse is from Romans 1:16.
"For I am not ashamed of the **Gospel** *of Jesus Christ, for it is the power of God for salvation to everyone who believes, to the Jew first and also to the Greek."*

#3963

Pistis

PEACE-teace

Πίστις

Pistis is a noun which means "faith," "faithfulness" or "trust." *Pistis* is almost always translated "faith." Before New Testament times, this word meant the trust one man put in another in a friendship, a business relationship or in lending money or property. It could also mean the trust man put in pagan gods. This trust was not firm, however. According to mythology, the gods were a jealous and devious lot. To remember this word think of a President having faith that his ambassador can bring peace to his warring nations.

The New Testament teaches that *pistis* is something we cannot do without. Faith (and not appeasing works) is what pleases God. It is impossible to please God without having faith (Hebrews 11:6).

In James we read that if we have faith, we will be doing the deeds that prove it (James 2:22).

In Hebrews 11:1, the Bible defines faith as knowing that what we hope for in God will happen, and that those eternal things which we cannot see actually exist. The exciting part is that we do not just have a mental belief that the eternal exists, but we actually have proof through our faith which God gives us. It is like finding the right answer in school; once you see it, you know it is right.

Studying chapter 11 of Hebrews is like a visit to the faith "hall-of-fame." What's more, most of the great people of faith listed in this chapter were just ordinary folks like you and me. Abraham was just a pagan shepherd when God called him. Then Abram (his original name) did one simple thing—he decided to believe that God was true to His Word. Because of this, God proclaimed him as righteous.

Our sample verse is from Hebrews 11:1.
*"Now **faith** is the substance of what is hoped for; the evidence of what is unseen."*

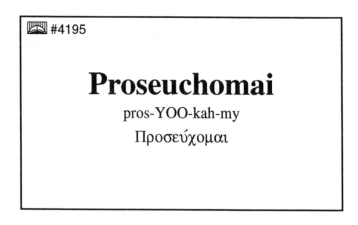

#4195

Proseuchomai

pros-YOO-kah-my

Προσεύχομαι

Proseuchomai is a verb which means "to pray." The original meaning was "to pray" as in the New Testament. However, the purpose and object of prayer to the pagan Greek was nothing like the exciting things that could happen to the New Testament Christian. The common Greek prayed to the pagan gods for help, favor, etc., but the prayer was offered in fear, rather than in expectation that his entreaty would be answered. The non-Christian would pray only to help himself. To help you recall the meaning of *proseuchomai*, think of a prisoner praying that a prosecutor will be merciful.

What a difference appears in the New Testament. Prayers are made to help the one praying, but many more prayers are made to help others, that God will be glorified. Prayer should exhibit our willingness to please God because of the love He gives.

Many of the occurrences of *proseuchomai* in the New Testament are in reference to Jesus or one of the apostles praying. Jesus often taught the importance and the how-to of prayer both in sermons and by example (Matthew 6:5-8). Certainly if Jesus saw the need to pray, all believers should be ready to do the same. The prayer Jesus taught his disciples (what is known as the Lord's Prayer) is found in Luke 11:2-4 and Matthew 6:9-13.

The apostle Paul also admonished believers to pray. What is great about the prayers of the saints is that their petitions are heard by Someone who can and wants to answer. Some of the reasons given for praying in the Bible are: to move the heart of God through persistent prayer (see Luke 18:1-8 for this important parable); to receive guidance: to avoid evil (Luke 22:46); and to communicate with God (Matthew 6:6).

Our sample verse is from 1 Thessalonians 5:17. *"**Pray** without ceasing."*

📖 #3390

Nikao

nee-KAH-oh

Νικάω

Nikao is a verb which means "to overcome" or "to be victorious." You have probably heard the word "nike" in advertisements about various products. "Nike" is a specific form of this word *nikao*. The ancient Greeks used this word to talk about superiority of persons or armies. It was used as a military word and as a civilian word in the sense of personal victories. The Greeks even had a goddess of superiority, named Nike, who might help to overcome an opponent.

In the New Testament, *nikao* gets really exciting. Being an overcomer in the kingdom of God is something extra special. In fact, Paul thought it was super. He made a compound word by adding *huper* (which translated into English is "hyper" or "super") to *nikao*. The King James Version says "we are more than conquerors." With the help of this Greek word, Paul was saying we are super-victors! See Romans 8:37 for this famous Scripture. Previously, in Romans 3:4, Paul used the word *nikao* when stating that no one can overcome God. Then in chapter 8, Paul lets us know that God is on our side.

Most of the uses of *nikao* are in Revelation. In the first part of that Book, we see all the great things that are promised to the one who overcomes until the end (like being able to rule over nations and having a stone inscribed with a secret name). The best part about overcoming is that it is part of being a Christian—it is something we **are**!

Our sample verse is from Revelation 12:11. *"They* **overcame** *him by the blood of the Lamb and the word of their testimony."*

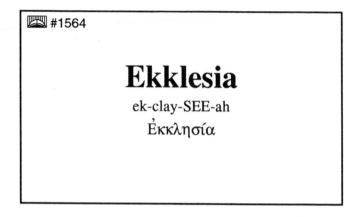

#1564

Ekklesia

ek-clay-SEE-ah

Ἐκκλησία

Ekklesia is the noun from which we get our English adjective, "ecclesiastical." *Ekklesia* may be translated "assembly," "congregation" or "church." Remember that Ecclesiastes is the Greek name for the Old Testament Book of wisdom literature which was written by a preacher. This should help you remember the meaning of *ekklesia*. Originally, this word was used to mean a council or tribunal which served as the court system for a city.

While *ekklesia* literally means "called out," this is not exactly the meaning used in the New Testament. The proper concept for this word is the congregation of believers or what we today call a church. Since the church is called out of the world of sin, *ekklesia* is a term which fits the church well. *Ekklesia* can refer to a local body of believers such as in 1 Corinthians 11:18 or the entire group of believers in the world, most dynamically referred to in Matthew 16:18.

Many people believe that the seven churches in Revelation 1-3 describe seven types of churches either today or throughout history. This is possible without discrediting that John was writing to actual local assemblies in his time. As you read Revelation 1-3, keep in mind that John was writing to particular churches at that time, but the message is still valid for today.

Our sample verse is from Matthew 16:18.
"I will build My **church**, *and the gates of hell will not prevail against it."*

📖 #2057

Eschatos

ES-cah-toss

῎Εσχατος

Eschatos is an adjective which means "last," "end" or "final." Originally the word had a basic and simple meaning. While this natural meaning is sometimes used in the Bible, a further and greater meaning is attached. Much teaching is given on the "end times" or what scholars call eschatology which is the study of last things. The beginning of the word *eschatos* is like the beginning of the word "escape." To remember this word think about escaping from all of the judgments in the book of Revelation—a book of the end times.

Almost without exception, this Greek word is used in reference to the last days or the end of the world. The main passages for study in this area in the New Testament are Matthew 24 and 25 and Revelation 4-21.

Another teaching employing the word *eschatos* concerns humility. Jesus says to take the last place when going to a banquet. Jesus explained that taking the position of humility will bring honor later (Luke 14:9-11). The greatest men of God were considered last or the most insignificant according to the world's measurement.

A saying of Jesus that many find confusing is "the first shall be last and the last first" (Matthew 19:30). It may be confusing because it is often quoted without the surrounding context of the verse. In this section of Matthew, Jesus is speaking of the Gentiles receiving salvation. Many Gentiles entered the kingdom first even though they were the last to hear the Word of God.

Our sample verse is from 2 Timothy 3:1.
*"But realize this, that in the **last** days*
difficult times will come."

⌨ #3814

Parousia

pah-roo-SEE-ah

Παρουσία

Parousia is a noun which can mean "coming," "advent" or "presence." In ancient Greece this word referred to someone's wealth or any great possession or sometimes even an army. Most of the time, though, *parousia* meant the arrival of someone or something. Hundreds of examples of this meaning occur in secular Greek.

It is particularly interesting to note that this word often referred to the coming of royalty, a pagan god visiting the earth disguised as a man, or some V.I.P. coming to town. This paved the way for the usage of *parousia* in the New Testament. Think of a window shopper coming to "peruse" the sale items in a store to help you remember the meaning of *parousia*.

Most of the occurrences of this Greek word in the New Testament are in Paul's letters, and all but six of the 24 times *parousia* is used refer to Christ's coming. Even though this particular Greek word doesn't occur often, the idea behind the word is not only important, but spectacular.

The tremendous doctrine of Jesus' second coming can be found in Matthew 24 and the Book of 1 Thessalonians. In Matthew 24 Jesus is teaching on His second coming. The main idea is that it will be an event so sudden that preparation must be made ahead of time. In 1 Thessalonians, Paul corrects a false teaching that had been going around the church concerning the second coming of Jesus. The church actually had been convinced that the Christians who had died would miss out on the great event. Paul let them know this was not the case. It is fascinating that the word "rapture" refers to the doctrine of Christ's second return, yet the word itself does not occur in the Bible. The idea behind the word "rapture," however, comes from the meaning of *parousia*—the "catching away" of the saints at the coming of the Lord.

Our sample verse is from James 5:8.
*"And be patient; establish your hearts
because the **coming** of the Lord is near."*

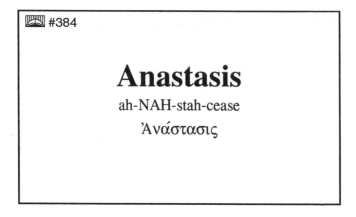

#384

Anastasis

ah-NAH-stah-cease

Ἀνάστασις

Anastasis is a noun which means "resurrection" or "rising." It is one of two words used for resurrection and is used primarily to refer to resurrection from the dead.

Originally, this word was also used for someone standing up or rising from a night's sleep. In the New Testament, however there is only one case where *anastasis* does not refer to someone rising from the dead (Luke 2:34). The New Testament puts a different meaning on this Greek word than the ancient Greeks.

A powerful moment in Jesus' ministry on earth was the raising of Lazarus from the dead. You can find this event recorded in John 11. Before Jesus raised Lazarus from the dead, He commented that

Lazarus was only sleeping. Then, at Jesus' command, Lazarus rose up from his four-day "nap."
 To help you remember the meaning of *anastasis*, recall that the most important job of an anesthesiologist is to raise up the patient after surgery.

Surprisingly, the word *anastasis* rarely refers to the resurrection of Jesus, but usually refers to the saints rising at the second coming (e.g., Matthew 22:30-32). Paul tells us that the resurrection is the basis for the preaching of the gospel in 1 Corinthians 15. *Anastasis* was a simple word the ancient Greeks used to mean "standing up." But in the New Testament, this word is "reborn" to mean "resurrection" from the dead.

Our sample verse is from John 11:25.
"Jesus said, 'I am the **resurrection** *and the life.'"*

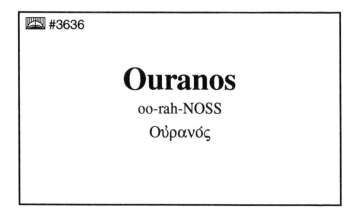

#3636

Ouranos

oo-rah-NOSS

Οὐρανός

Ouranos is the Greek word for "heaven." As you might expect, this word occurs hundreds of times and in nearly every Book of the New Testament.

In early times, the Greeks used *ouranos* to refer to the sky above the earth or outer space—the starry sky of the milky way. They also used this word when speaking of the home of their mythological gods. Uranus was often referred to specifically when the Greeks talked about heaven because they believed that he was the god of the sky. As you may have already realized, this is where we get our name for the planet Uranus.

The Bible views heaven in three parts instead of two. The New Testament uses *ouranos* to refer to the sky (Luke 12:56), outer space (Matthew 24:29) and the throne of God (Ephesians 6:9). But there is another more magnetic use of this Greek word.

Jesus often used the phrase, "the kingdom of heaven." When Jesus said this, He was not talking about a physical place. Instead, He was directing the people's attention toward the rule of God which should be in their hearts. The first time *ouranos* is mentioned in the New Testament it is used in this way (Matthew 3:2). Many times Jesus said that He was from heaven (John 6:51), therefore His message is the truth. For those who do believe, a new heaven and earth are being prepared. God did not give up on His original plan for man to live in paradise. One day, all will be restored.

Our sample verse is from Revelation 21:1. *"I saw a new* **heaven** *and a new earth, the first* **heaven** *and earth had passed away."*

A FINAL WORD

Now it is time to for you to discover the secret of why these 25 Greek words are so amazing. Because you learned them, you now possess the building blocks for a deeper understanding of your Bible. You may have noticed that the words were grouped by subject, and that these groups were in turn placed in a biblically ordered sequence.

With *25 Amazing Greek Words* you have discovered the most basic biblical truths. The trinity, **God** the **Father,** the **Lord Jesus Christ** and the Holy **Spirit** cooperated to create the **world, angels** and **man.** After this, Adam **sinned** and deserved **death** and therefore needed a way of **salvation.** God **loved** man so much that He provided that way by a **blood covenant** which was ultimately fulfilled by Jesus Christ, entitling Him to be Lord over all.

The **Scripture** tells us the **Gospel** is the "good news" about this provision which is available to everyone. Once we receive the Gospel, we have **gained victory.** We now live by **faith, pray** to God and meet together with other believers in a local **assembly** to promote His kingdom. At the **end** of time, all believers will be **caught up** to meet the Lord. Christians who have already died will be **resurrected** with the same power that raised Jesus. As overcomers, they will receive their eternal reward in **heaven.**

Your Bible study is empowered when you understand the framework of God's Word. As you learn more about your Bible, you will discover that any new information links together and fits within this simple 25 word structure that you already know. Within these 25 words, you have the foundation of what Bible scholars call "systematic theology."

You are to be commended for reading this book, because it shows that you desire to know more of God's Word. You have practiced the key verse of all Bible studies:

"Do your best to present yourself to God as one approved, a craftsman who need not be ashamed but who properly handles the word of truth" (2 Timothy 2:15).

Scope of 25 Amazing Greek Words
The Framework of Systematic Theology

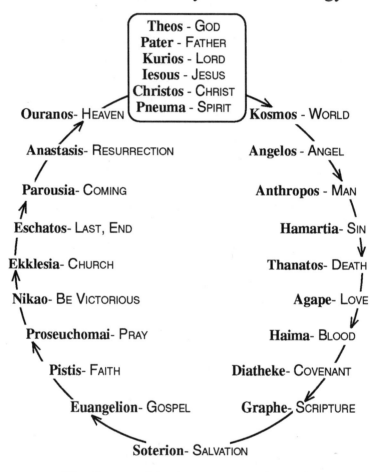

Theos - God
Pater - Father
Kurios - Lord
Iesous - Jesus
Christos - Christ
Pneuma - Spirit

Ouranos- Heaven

Anastasis- Resurrection

Parousia- Coming

Eschatos- Last, End

Ekklesia- Church

Nikao- Be Victorious

Proseuchomai- Pray

Pistis- Faith

Euangelion- Gospel

Kosmos - World

Angelos - Angel

Anthropos - Man

Hamartia- Sin

Thanatos- Death

Agape- Love

Haima- Blood

Diatheke- Covenant

Graphe- Scripture

Soterion- Salvation

The Secret of *25 Amazing Greek Words*

Within this chart lies the foundation of biblical understanding. The Greek New Testament was written with a vocabulary of 5,457 words. Every one of them has its logical place in this chart, which demonstrates the unbreakable chain of faith.

Use *25 Amazing Greek Words* with
Any Good Bible Study or Reference Tool

To get the most out of *25 Amazing Greek Words*, use it with any other Bible study tool. The best companion resource this author can recommend is a remarkable 16-volume Bible study tool called **The Complete Biblical Library** available from the publisher of this book, World Library Press, Inc.

If you enjoyed *25 Amazing Greek Words* you should know that **The Complete Biblical Library** offers a powerful word study on every Greek word in the New Testament. This amazing Bible study tool has been acclaimed by some of today's leading Bible scholars as the most useful of this century because of its comprehensiveness and usability. **The Complete Biblical Library** lays open the New Testament to any curious Bible student in an understandable and easy to use way. Anyone can study from the ground text of the New Testament quickly and accurately, without any previous knowledge of Greek necessary.

World Library Press has made **The Complete Biblical Library** affordable to everyone through a simple plan. For more information on **The Complete Biblical Library** call World Library Press weekdays, 8-5 CT, Toll-Free, at **1-800-446-6238** Ext. U62.

Or write to: 📖 **World Library Press**
2274 East Sunshine Street • Dept. U6B
Springfield, Missouri   65804

World Library Press
2274 East Sunshine Street • Dept. U6B
Springfield, Missouri 65804
1-800-446-6238 Ext. U62